REACHING FOR THE STARS

DAN JANSEN
Olympic Speedskating Champion

Bob Italia

Published by Abdo & Daughters, 4940 Viking Drive, Suite 622, Edina, Minnesota 55435

Library bound edition distributed by Rockbottom Books, Pentagon Tower, P.O. Box 36036, Minneapolis, Minnesota 55435

Printed in the United States

Cover Photo credit: Bettmann
Interior Photo credits: Bettmann

Edited by Rosemary Wallner

Library of Congress Cataloging-in-Publication Data

Italia, Bob, 1955-
        Dan Jansen : Olympic champion / Bob Italia.
                p.   cm. -- (Reaching For The Stars)
        ISBN 1-56239-340-5
        1. Jansen, Dan --Juvenile literature. 2. Skaters--
        United States--Juvenile literature. I. Title.   II. Series.
        GV850.J36I82   1994
        796.9'14'092--dc20   94-35020
        [B]   CIP
                                                                                 AC

TABLE OF CONTENTS

GREAT EXPECTATIONS

He was one of the best U.S. speedskaters ever. At 22 years of age, he had easily won the 500-meter race in World Sprint Championships. Grabbing two gold medals in the Olympics a week later was supposed to be a breeze. But hours before the first big race, something happened to Dan Jansen that would forever change his life, and turn his gold-medal dreams into a six-year struggle for glory and vindication.

Dan Jansen's story is about more than winning a medal. It is about dealing with the death of a loved one, overcoming a tragedy, and persevering to the end. Though he never quite lived up to the greatest expectations, Jansen's single gold-medal victory will remain one of the most dramatic triumphs in Olympic history.

At the 1994 Winter Games, speedskater Dan Jansen set a world record in the men's Olympic 1,000 meter event.

5

LEARNING TO SKATE

Dan Jansen grew up in West Allis, Wisconsin, a block from the old site of the annual North American Speedskating Championships. He was the youngest of police lieutenant Harry and nurse Gerry Jansen's nine children.

Speedskating was a Jansen family affair. "We couldn't afford a babysitter, so we took the little ones along as well," said Harry, who laced Jansen into a pair of double-runners at age 4.

According to Harry, Jansen was at first "no better than anyone else in the family. He had wobbly ankles and had to work very hard on them."

The hard work paid off. When he was eight years old, Jansen began winning regional meets. At age 12, Jansen began winning national meets. In 1984, he was picked for the Olympics. He placed fourth in the 500-meter race at Sarajevo, Yugoslavia.

"I was 18," Jansen said, "and I just missed a bronze medal. I was so excited. Then I came home, and the reporters were saying, That's too bad [about finishing fourth].' That's when I started to feel there's too much emphasis on medals."

It was a great accomplishment, but there was little time to celebrate. Jansen had to prepare for the 1988 Olympic Winter Games in Calgary, Alberta, Canada.

The tune-up came in 1986 at the World Cup Championships. Jansen breezed past the competition in the 500 and the 1,000. Then a week before the Olympics, Jansen won the 500-meters at the World Sprint Championships in his home town of West Allis, Wisconsin. Jansen was at top form. The Olympic gold medal seemed like a formality.

THE 1988 OLYMPICS

The 1988 Olympic speedskating competition was reaching dizzying new speeds. Before Jansen skated, two skaters broke Eric Heiden's old record. The 500-meter race should have been the biggest day of Jansen's life, but it ended up being the worst.

On Feb. 14, Jansen, then 22, was ready to compete for the gold. But at 6 A.M. he was roused from bed by his brother Mike. He was calling from Wisconsin, saying their sister Jane, 27—who had been waging a year-long battle with leukemia—was dying and wanted to say goodbye.

Jane had been married for five years to West Allis fireman Rich Beres. She first learned she had cancer in January 1987, 24 hours after the birth of her third child. The doctors suggested a bone-marrow transplant. Jansen and another of his sisters, Joanne, were the only ones whose bone marrow matched Jane's. Jansen was prepared to go ahead with the procedure. But Jane felt it would weaken him and put him out of the Olympics. So she said no. Instead she accepted the gift of marrow from Joanne, who was a slightly better match.

For a time after the September procedure, Jane seemed to rally. Then she reentered the hospital. Just days before the Olympics, Jane was featured in a TV special in which she tearfully acknowledged her brother's devotion.

"I want to go out there and do well for her because she's fought so hard," Jansen told one newspaper.

A speedskater herself, Jane had urged Jansen to go to Calgary despite her deteriorating health. While Mike held the phone to her ear, Jansen spoke to Jane. But she was on a respirator and could not reply. Before they hung up, Jansen asked Mike to give her a kiss for him, and he did.

Dan didn't go back to sleep after talking to Jane. Later he went to an early lunch with Henriksen. When Jansen returned from lunch, he found a slip of paper. "I've got a message," he told Henriksen. "But I don't think I want to know what it is."

Jane had been pronounced dead at 8:50 a.m., Calgary time, less than three hours after Dan had spoken to her.

Henriksen called a U.S. speedskating team meeting for about 2:30. There Jansen's teammates said that they would dedicate the Games to Jane. "It seemed to buoy his spirits a little bit," said Mike Crowe, the U.S. coach.

In the hours before the race, the ABC-TV cameras followed Jansen as he practiced grimly on the Olympic oval. That evening, as American TV viewers looked on transfixed, Jansen stepped up to the starting line for the 500-meter sprint.

As the starter raised his gun, Jansen jumped out, committing a false start—something he rarely does. Then, barely 10 seconds into the race, he fell, sliding helplessly across the ice. He tripped a Japanese skater before crashing into the foam cushion that lined the rink.

Four days later, still burdened with grief, Jansen skated in the 1,000-meter race and had a record-setting pace through the first 800 meters. Then he fell again.

"At the time," remembered Jansen, "I was more concerned about my sister than I was about skating. But now it's time for me to look ahead."

When he fell the second time, on the straight-away of the 1,000-meter event, just 200 meters short of the finish, it was even more stunning. Watching from the gallery, brother Mike had just assured a sister, "Dan's made it through the toughest turns. He's fine now."

At the 600-meter mark, Jansen was .31 seconds faster than any of the competition. Then his right skate "caught an edge"— hit the ice on the side instead of the bottom of the blade—sending him to his hands and knees and into a wall. For a moment he sat on the ice, unbelieving. Then coach Mike Crowe and teammate Nick Thometz came over to help him off. Arriving at the bench area, he embraced his fiancee, Canadian speedskater Natalie Grenier, and sobbed.

Speedskater Dan Jansen is disqualified after crashing in the 500 meters race in the 1988 Winter Olympics.

Later, Harry Jansen said, "I think he was thinking about Jane. I knew he'd either fall or he'd skate the race of his life."

Jansen's mother Gerry had seen the race on TV. She spoke for the millions who watched at home and in Calgary, where a cheering crowd fell into shocked silence: "I think we were all just kind of numb."

Jansen flew home by private jet to attend his sister's funeral. "We hugged and we cried," said Mrs. Jansen. "My daughter's death has now become more of a reality to him."

Later that day Jansen visited his sister's husband and her three young children. He gave them his Olympic participant's medal. At home the postman kept bringing carts of mail full of sympathy and admiration.

THE 1992 OLYMPICS

Jansen, now 26, looked forward to the Olympics in Albertville, France. Once again, Jansen was positioned for a gold medal. Months earlier, Jansen had tied for first in the 500 meters race at a World Cup meet in Berlin. His toughest competition was expected to be Germany's Uwe-Jens Mey, the 1988 Olympic champion in the 500.

A 190-lb. six-footer, Jansen, according to his new coach, Peter Mueller, was neither the biggest nor the strongest skater. Nor, added Mueller, was he any faster than some of the others. But Jansen had something extra. "He is mentally tough," said Mueller. "He knew he's going to win every time he goes out there."

Redemption did not come, as everyone hoped, in Albertville. When Jansen lost his balance in a turn and finished in fourth place in the 500, questions, quickly followed by opinions, took form. Eric Heiden never fell. Bonnie Blair never fell. Maybe Jansen was jinxed, hexed, doomed. The doomsayers seemed right when Jansen staggered home 26th in the 1000. Was he finished as an Olympic skater? Some people thought so. Jansen began wondering himself. But then he decided to work even harder for the next Olympics.

GETTING READY. . .AGAIN

Jansen did a great deal of work on the 1,000, both mentally and physically, in the two years since Albertville. He consulted with Florida sports psychologist Jim Loehr, who had worked with a number of elite athletes who seemed jinxed. His clients included Gabriela Sabatini, who won a U.S. Open title in 1990 with Loehr's help by overcoming her fear of coming to the net.

Loehr urged Jansen not to specialize solely in the 500. He convinced him that a skater who threw so much of himself into so tense and short a race only manufactured pressure and tempted failure.

Before turning in each night for the past two years, Jansen filled out a worksheet to help him set goals. At the top of each sheet he wrote, "I love the 1,000."

"I could open up to 600 meters, but I'd run out of gas in the last lap," Jansen said. So Mueller worked with Jansen on his conditioning. Together he and Loehr turned Jansen from a skater who dreaded the longer sprint into one who looked forward to it.

THE 1993 WORLD CUP

On December 4, Jansen became the first speedskater to break the 36-second barrier in the 500 meters when he won a World Cup race at the Viking ship hall in Hamar, Norway, in the time of 35.92. "To look up and see 35 was something I'd dreamed of for a long time," said Jansen.

Five days later Jansen was back home at the new Olympic speedskating training oval in Milwaukee for the U.S. Speedskating Federation Media Day. Michael Bauman of *The Milwaukee Journal* began his questioning of Jansen this way: "Dan, you've won everything in speedskating but one thing...." A smiling Jansen interrupted: "And what would that happen to be, Mike?" That would happen to be one of those shiny gold things that Olympic winners wear around their necks.

Lillehammer would be the 28-year-old Jansen's fourth and probably last shot at a gold medal. He was only 18 when he finished fourth in the 500 at Sarajevo in '84, a mere .16 off the bronze metal performance. At the '92 Games, Jansen finished fourth in the 500 and 26th in the 1,000, partly because his

Dan Jansen decided to change from skating the 500-meter to skating the 1,000-meter when he entered the 1994 Winter Olympics.

muscular body was too heavy for the soft ice of Albertville's outdoor oval and partly because he was weighed down by memories of Calgary.

But with Lillehammer only two months away, Jansen was skating as never before. In Hamar, two days after breaking the world record of 36.02 in the 500, which he himself had set last March at a meet in Calgary, Jansen established a track record in the 1,000. His time of 1:13.01 was only .03 off the world record.

After breaking the world record in the 500, Jansen had immediately skated over to his coach, Peter Mueller, and said, "There's more in there." Mueller, who won the gold in the 1,000 at the '76 Olympics, began working with Jansen in May 1991 and was one reason that Jansen was racing so well. The coach had stoked Jansen's competitive fire and particularly had changed his approach to the 1,000. Jansen was no longer trying to skate the 1,000 the same way he did the 500—all out from start to finish.

Said Jansen, "Peter has taught me how to skate the 1,000. I've learned how to skate at not quite top speed and do it under control, which is what you have to do if you want to have anything left for the last lap. I definitely have twice as good a chance for a medal in the 1,000. The 1,000 has become fun."

Jansen was helped by the arrival on May 27 of a baby girl, whom he and his wife, Robin, named after his sister. The seven-month-old Jane was in attendance at the Media Day press conference as Jansen said, "It changes my outlook on everything, of course. I can leave training, and leave it at the oval, knowing that Jane's going to be looking up at me when I get home."

Jansen sharpened his focus by limiting his time with the media. Apologizing at the press conference, he said, "Nothing against you guys, I like having you around, but it takes time . . . and I just don't want to hear those questions about the past anymore." In Lillehammer, Jansen would have a chance to silence those questions once and for all.

THE 1994 OLYMPICS

In the 500-meter race, Jansen's split time over the first 100 meters pleased him. He was his usual strong self in the backstretch. It was on the first stride of the last turn that he fleetingly lost control under his left skate. He tried to pull his foot back, but his left hand grazed the ice, and over so short a distance a lost half-second is a lost race.

His wife, Robin, knew instantly. "Why, God?" she asked herself as she watched from the stands. "Why again?"

And it was she who seemed to take the loss the hardest. She lashed out on Norwegian TV about the unusually hard ice. It didn't allow Jansen to dig in and use his power. The ice favored the slighter (5' 8 1/2", 163-pound) Aleksandr Golubev of Russia, who won the gold medal.

Mueller was more subdued. "As far as I'm concerned, he's the best," he said of Jansen. "He always will be in my book. If he skates 100 times, he's going to win 95. This doesn't take away from what he is—the greatest sprinter of all time and a gentleman."

Jansen faced the press after the loss in the 500. But then he saw his wife and parents. When he saw their disappointment, he realized he couldn't cope with the interview. "I feel so bad," he told his wife as they drove off from the press conference. "Those guys are just doing their jobs, and I should have talked to them."

When Jansen heard that an ESPN crew had waited two hours outside the hall for him in subzero temperatures, and that one cameraman had suffered frostbite on two fingers as a result, Jansen tapped out an apology on the Olympics-wide electronic mail system.

"I'm supposed to win, something goes wrong, and they can't celebrate," he said after the 500.

Jansen sought out Dale Hofmann of his hometown paper, *The Milwaukee Sentinel.* He told him, "Sorry, Milwaukee." He was still awake at three the next morning, blaming himself that Wisconsinites would be disappointed once again.

The scores of well-wishers only heightened his sense of carrying the hopes of others. "You want people to pull for you," he would say. "And it was good because you like to have support. But it was bad because I didn't want to disappoint people anymore."

LAST CHANCE FOR GLORY

The final act approached. Igor Zhelezovsky of Belarus was the favorite. Jansen had always skated his best 1,000 meters without much forethought. Besides, there wasn't much tinkering needed on his form. He had torn through a handtimed 1:12—equivalent to a world record—only a week earlier in training.

Jansen and his trainers agreed that they wouldn't excessively talk through the race. And Jansen wouldn't go through his usual visualization techniques each night before going to sleep. Jansen would simply skate.

But when he took to the ice on Friday, Jansen felt funny. His timing was off. He struggled for traction. So he pedaled two hard sprints on an exercise bike to bring his legs to life. And he reversed his decision not to skate hard.

Jansen laid down a swift 16.71 over the first 200 meters. The man he was paired with, Junichi Inoue of Japan, had come out fast too. So at the 400-meter mark, where the skaters cross over from one lane to the other, Jansen was able to ride briefly in Inoue's slipstream and slingshot into the next turn. Here Robin actually dared feel good as she watched with Jane. Dan wasn't working too hard. "He was smooth as glass," she said later.

But Jansen being Jansen, it was only a question of where danger would strike. It jumped him on the next-to-last turn. He skated in the inner lane, where the turn was tighter, the G forces greater and the risk of a fall keener. He was tiring, too, but this time when he slipped, his left hand barely grazed the ice. He lost two or three hundredths of a second, yet he kept his rhythm. "For some reason I was calm about it," Jansen said. "I told myself that if I tried to get back too fast, I would slip again."

*Jansen skated the 1,000-meter race at Hamar
smoother than he had in the past.*

On the next straight-away, his coach nearly clapped Jansen on the back out of excitement. He finished in 1:12.43, beating out Zhelezovsky, who won the silver medal, and Russia's Sergei Klevchenya, who took the bronze. The man the press was calling "the Bill Buckner of winter" a few days earlier had suddenly turned into Superman. "The slip, he just skated through it," Mueller would say later. "This time the man upstairs took care of him."

"Maybe he did," Jansen added. "Or maybe Jane had something to do with it."

Maybe it was his sister Jane who skated for Jansen this time. Or maybe Robin had. Hyperventilating, she rushed to get treatment from an emergency medical technician after the race. Everyone else in the hall seemed flushed, as if they, too, had just gone 1,000 meters.

The joy wasn't just for the Americans. It was shared by people of every nationality—particularly citizens of Norway and Holland, where speedskating is a major sport.

"There is something in his eyes that tells you he is honest," said Ben van der Burg, a former Dutch 1,500-meter champ who had watched Jansen on the circuit for years. "They are faithful eyes, like a big Labrador dog. To do what he did—six tenths of a second under his personal best—is unbelievable. To do it here is even more unbelievable."

Suddenly, all the previous failures seemed to have a meaning. Even the disaster in the 500 meters seemed to be part of the grand plan.

Jansen had won the 1,000 meters in world-record time. In doing so, he ended a decade-long saga of Olympic expectation and futility that was known the world over. Now the burden had been lifted.

But Jansen's victory was more than relief. It was vindication. A gold medal now hung from Jansen's neck, and not even Bonnie Blair's historic gold in the women's 500 a day later—she became the first U.S. athlete to win the same event in three consecutive Winter Games—could eclipse Jansen's breakthrough.

In seven previous Olympic races, Jansen had never really skated for a medal. He had always skated for other people. He had skated for his sister Jane. He had skated for his parents.

Dan Jansen is jubilant after setting a new world record in the 1,000-meter speedskating event at the 1994 Winter Olympics.

He skated for his wife and their nine-month-old daughter. He had skated for his coach, and for all the people back in Wisconsin who have never lost faith that he would ultimately win.

Yet Jansen ultimately won not by seizing something boldly for himself, but by expecting so very little.

"The way I got relaxed was not to care," Jansen explained. "No matter what happened in the 1,000, my family wasn't going to be gone. And losing the 1,000 wouldn't be as big a shock as not winning the 500. I went in with such low expectations because I didn't want to set myself up for disappointment."

RECEIVING THE MEDAL

By winning so many gold medals, fellow Olympian Bonnie Blair had become comfortable on the podium. She happily sang along when the U. S. national anthem was played.

But Jansen was not familiar with his position on the podium. All he could do was mouth the words. He wanted this medal ceremony to last forever.

This golden moment had been so long in coming. And at 28, he was almost certainly competing in his last Olympic race.

His eyes began to fill up. At "gave proof through the night," he blinked, sending a tear down his face. Jansen didn't want it to, but the anthem was ending. So he turned his eyes upward and saluted his sister. "Finally I feel I've made other people happy instead of having them feel sorry for me," he said later.

U.S. speedskater Dan Jansen shows off his gold medal for the men's 1,000-meter race at the 1994 Winter Olympics.

THE VICTORY LAP

After descending the podium, Jansen skated a victory lap. The crowd in the *Vikingskipet* cheered and applauded. A security guard passed little Jane over the heads of stunned photographers and into her daddy's arms. With the arena dark and the spotlight illuminating him, Jane's father carried her once around the rink as a waltz played on.

At the following press conference, the emcee asked the media for a round of applause. The media—who had for years been nipping at his heels—actually provided it. The runners-up seemed almost happy that they had lost.

As Jane teethed on her dad's gold medal, Jansen said he was so happy for Robin. Robin said she was so happy for Jansen. President Clinton called, and moments later Hillary called. Then the emcee read poetry. "I remember your poet, Robert Frost," he told Jansen. "He said, 'Nothing gold can stay.' But you who know what it means to have lost, can really stay gold today."

The words weren't entirely appropriate.   This gold so long in coming would linger for a long, long time.

Jansen does a victory lap carrying his new daughter, Jane.

Jansen said that he was thinking about returning to school to study marketing and, eventually, coaching kids. "But," he said, "I don't really want to plan the rest of my life. I just want to enjoy the moment and spend some time with my family."

When he returned to Milwaukee, Jansen made clear just how important family was to him. Called up onto a stage to address a cheering throng of 1,000 fans at the airport, Jansen expressed his gratitude and, announcing "Here it is," pulled the gold medal from his jeans pocket. Then Robin handed Jane to him, and Jansen—American flag in one hand, daughter in the other—strode triumphantly offstage. A giggling Robin had to remind Dan that he'd left something behind—the gold medal.

LIFE AFTER SKATING

Following the Olympics, Jansen entered the speedskating World Cup in the Netherlands in March. There, he won the overall gold medal.

On August 24, 1994, Dan Jansen announced his retirement from speedskating. Having finally won the elusive Olympic gold medal, Jansen had become busy with endorsements and a new career as a TV commentator.

Jansen joined CBS-TV in June 1994. He reported on winter-related sports for the network's weekend series "Eye On Sports."

"I have accomplished all that I can in my sport," Jansen said. "I will miss it, especially the competition. But I am looking for-ward to spending more time with my family."

Jansen may miss the competition, but speedskating fans around the world will miss him even more. Rarely does a sport produce such a noble champion.